# Kathleen's Secrets

# For An Adequate

# Lifestyle

## A Guide For Living the
## Good Enough Life

# Kathleen's Secrets For An Adequate Lifestyle

## A Guide For Living the Good Enough Life

### Kathleen F. Rhodes

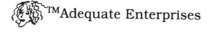

™Adequate Enterprises

Manufactured in the United States of America
Library of Congress Catalog Card Number:  98-96839
ISBN:  0-9667934-0-4
Illustrations:  Kim Harlow
Cover design:  Diane Richards
Page layout:  Bob Fields

**Library of Congress Cataloging-in-Publication Data**

Rhodes, Kathleen F. (Kathleen Flanigan)
Kathleen's secrets for an adequate lifestyle:  a guide for living the good enough life / Kathleen F. Rhodes

ISBN 0-9667934-0-4 (pbk.)
 1.  Humor — United States
 I.  Rhodes, Kathleen F., 1951 -    , II.  Title

                              **CIP**
                          98-96839

  Adequate Enterprises
   12964 Portsmouth Dr.
   Carmel, Indiana  46032


       Visit our website:  www.adequate.net
       Email address:  kathleen@adequate.net

To Emily, who suggested it; Rachel, who inspired it; and Michael, who encouraged, loved and nurtured it; and to adequacy seekers everywhere who need it, this book is dedicated.

# Contents

## Secrets For An Adequate Lifestyle
### A Guide For Living the Good Enough Life

## Other Thoughts

# Preface

*. . . how I learned to stop whining and love my
imperfections.*

One day (a Friday, I believe) my daughter and I
were frantically rushing around, trying to get our
house ready for a potential buyer.  Time was short
and we used some rather unorthodox methods of
housekeeping in order to get it all done.  My daughter
suggested that I write some of these methods down as
hints for other people who may find themselves in a
similar situation.  I agreed.  I believe that there are
probably many out there whose life habits are as
haphazard as mine and who, like me, feel incredibly
guilty and inadequate.  This idea became my first

article: "How To Sell Your House." I found it extremely cathartic and those who read it seemed to enjoy it, so I kept writing. It occurred to me that in these nervous, modern times, we use an incredible amount of energy striving to be perfect — as spouses, as parents, in our jobs, fitness routines, daily schedules, etc. Yet everywhere we look we are being told just how inadequate we are (pick up any women's magazine published, peruse the bookstores' self-help aisles). I decided it was time for us to begin a movement toward adequacy. Simple adequacy. Let us celebrate the Adequate Lifestyle! We need to stop beating ourselves up because we're not and never will be anywhere near Martha Stewart perfect. Let's rediscover the joy in living life and relinquish the pressures of living "a perfect life." We must allow ourselves to be fallible, imperfect, funny, endearing human beings. This became my quest.

The next step in my journey to embracing adequacy was in 1996. I was given the opportunity to sing on a local radio program that showcased a variety of talent, spoken as well as musical. At the time I was singing in an all-girl group called "Hot Flash" (our motto: "It's not a medical condition, it's an *attitude*"). When I asked if I could perform one of my essays, they were enthusiastic — as long as I also showcased my talent for buying the pizza that night.

"Kathleen's Secrets For An Adequate Lifestyle" was created.

Through the research of the Center For Adequate Living (a fictitious non-profit, non-funded, non-organization), I provide valuable advice to those who are seeking relief from their hectic, search-for-perfection, guilt-ridden, technologically over-loaded, modern lives. *Our* motto is "Good Enough *Is* Good Enough!" This is a collection of the "Adequacy Reports" that were presented on the radio show, some articles that were published in *Indianapolis Woman* magazine, a couple that were featured in *The Indianapolis Star*, and others (including "How To Sell Your House") which have not yet reached beyond kith and kin.

This book is for those of you with the sinking feeling that you are losing the fight for perfection. Are you an adequacy seeker? Do fashion magazines depress you? Do you suffer from an acute case of internet-phobia? Are all of those self-help books mocking you from your bookshelf? And are you beginning to feel that you just can't take it anymore? Well, don't get mad . . . get *adequate!* Enjoy. And have an adequate day.

Kathleen F. Rhodes

# Secrets For An Adequate Lifestyle

## A Guide For Living the Good Enough Life

# Laundry

*. . . the secret to creating a perfect life — like maintaining control of our utility room — is a most illusive thing.*

$\mathcal{A}$dequacy seekers . . . our first research topic for adequate living is: laundry. We at the Center For Adequate Living feel that laundry is by far the lowest, most demeaning and onerous task inflicted upon the domestic human animal. This conclusion is based on our research that has shown that, no matter how much time is put in, how much energy and effort is expended, laundry is *never finished!* It is there, in the utility room, waiting, watching, knowing that after you've carefully folded the last towel and put it away, after the last crisp,

1

clean sheet has been spread lovingly on the last bed, you will walk past the utility room and, there, piled four feet high in the baskets will be more dirty laundry, much of which will have tags that mock you with "handwash separately in cold water; hang dry."

Where does this come from? What malevolent force is behind this laundry hell? What have we done to deserve "dry clean only?" We were scrupulously taught by our parents that the key to a happy, harmonious household is constant clean sheets and underwear. To neglect this crucial domestic duty would reveal us to the world as considerably less than adequate homemakers. We may have come a long way, babies, but there is a small, incessant voice that still haunts us. We know this voice — a voice from long ago. We can hear it in our dreams — "ring-around-the-collar!" So we often find ourselves in a panic, trying vainly to burrow through the accumulation and get control of our homes and, thus, our lives.

We at the Center For Adequate Living can help! We have developed the following laundry tips to make this stressful activity less so:

1. Choose one day each week for doing laundry. If that day passes and the laundry for some reason did not get done, do not allow yourself to do laundry until that day next week. You'd be amazed at how much time this rule has saved us at the

Center.  Although, after a couple of weeks, we are no longer asked out for lunch as much — which saves us money!

2. Don't let the laundry pile up.  Keep unsightly (and very likely unsanitary) dirty clothes out of sight. We put ours in the trunk of our car!

3. Never "hand wash separately in cold water."  Put everything together, wash in warm soapy water, and dry in dryer.  Those wimpy items that can't take it deserve what happens to them!

4. Keep a drawer for "socks without partners."  Every couple of months, dump the drawer into the trash. Do not attempt to match socks.

5. Be extremely careful when using certain laundry chemicals for especially soiled items.  We recommend kerosene *or* gasoline, *not both.*  Either one will ignite most fabrics sufficiently.

We know if you follow our suggestions, your life will be significantly more tranquil.  Smelly, but tranquil.  Have an adequate laundry day.

# Cooking

*. . . truly fine cooks possess many secrets,
none of which we know.*

$\mathcal{D}$o you struggle every day in the attempt to
get dinner on the table for your family?  We all want
to be innovative and creative with our cooking ideas.
We buy books and magazines that give us healthful
and delicious recipes and tempt us to try exotic food
items such as veal ("Not bad, tastes like beef") or
Cornish hen ("Not bad, tastes like chicken").  We try.
We really do.  And yet, somehow, our meals don't turn
out the way we hope.  Our ambitious efforts to create
the "perfect" meals are, alas, often thwarted through
no fault of our own.  Even with step-by-step instruc-

4

tions, our outcomes often tend to go awry. Let us give you an example.

The following is a meal plan from a book titled "Perfect Meals In Minutes." This particular meal plan provides the steps to prepare the dishes for a gourmet meal including: Broiled Fish Fillets with Lemon Butter, Green Beans in Peanut Sauce, and Noodles with Creamy Cheese Sauce. By following this simple plan we should be able to prepare this sumptuous meal for our family in a mere 30 minutes. Let's just see how our adequate household compares:

## Elegant Fish Dinner

### Perfect Meal Plan

### Adequate Plan

**7:00** Bring hot water to a boil in steamer for beans and in two-quart pan for noodles.

**7:00** Search for steamer. Discover that children have been using it to sift the sandbox. Decide to boil the beans in the two-quart pan. Look for another pan for noodles. Finding only two small sauce pans, bring water to boil in all pans.

**7:05** Wash and trim green beans, place in steamer. Heat.

**7:30** Wash and trim green beans, discarding any rotten, bug-infested, or dried out beans. Realizing that this process leaves only *five* edible beans, open two cans of green beans. Replace water with canned beans. Heat.

**7:10** Melt butter, mix with freshly squeezed lemon juice and, brush on fish. Arrange fish on broiling pan.

**7:45** Melt butter. Discover that the child you sent to the store for a lemon bought an apple instead because she doesn't *like* lemons. Brush fish with plain melted butter. Arrange on broiling pan. Husband indignantly informs you that this is the pan he uses to change the oil in the car. Discard fish and dig out frozen fish sticks.

**7:13** Boil noodles. Make sauce: Grate cheese and chop scallions, mix with milk and heat.

**8:00** Boil noodles. Start sauce. Find that your teenage son, having gone for many minutes without eating, has consumed the milk and cheese, and is heading for the frozen fish sticks. Banish son from kitchen. Explain to small daughter that scallions are *not* the deadly creatures found in the desert and she will *too* eat the noodles!

**7:18** Drain beans, mix with sauce. Place over warming dish.

**7:20** Broil fish, brush again with lemon butter, garnish with fresh dill from kitchen herb garden. Drain noodles, mix with sauce, place both over warming dish.

**7:25** Serve fish and side dishes with a loaf of warmed french bread. This meal is best served with a dry white wine.

**7:30** Accept well deserved accolades from family.

**8:20** Remember the cooking beans just as the smoke alarm goes off.

**8:35** Microwave fish sticks, garnish with cutting from Norfolk Island Pine (because you don't know where to get dill sprigs and who knows what they look like and nobody eats the garnish anyway).

**8:45** Serve fish sticks with over-cooked beans, plain noodles, and slices of white bread, if you have any. This meal is best served with two or three bottles of wine, any kind of wine.

**8:50** With well-practiced look, *dare* family to say a word!

Ah, dear adequacy seekers, do remember our culinary motto — good enough *is* good enough. Bon Appétit! Have an adequate evening meal.

# Feeding Our Children

*. . . wherein we learn that the secret to preserving our mental health is not necessarily healthy for our kids.*

 𝒫arents . . . What did your children have for breakfast today? For dinner last night? Are you even aware of their eating habits? Does this make you feel guilty? Do you despair because your children do not always eat the good, nutritious, wholesome food that you know they require in order to become the very best they can be? Do women's magazines chide you about the nutritional content of your children's daily food intake? Do you feel — let's face it — inadequate? Well, of course you do! Putting aside the assumption that it is the *intention* of most

8

women's magazines to make us feel guilty about practically everything we do, when they question our parenting skills, they are pushing a particularly sensitive button. Although we can handle (and usually agree with) their accusations that we are seriously deficient in our own love lives, fitness routines, fashion sense, career choices, behavior patterns, etc., when they imply that our children are at risk from our blatant inadequacies, well, that hurts! Whatever can we do? Aside from canceling our subscriptions to those magazines, of course; let's not do anything *too* drastic! Where can we turn to rescue our children from our own ineptitude? Where, indeed?

Take heart, dear seekers! We at the Center For Adequate Living are, as always, here for you! We have done extensive as well as exhaustive scientific research to discover the most adequate nutritional guidelines for producing highly adequate, nearly mature and mostly well-adjusted children. We have perused many, many "How to Feed Your Child" publications, some of which we went so far as to peruse while sitting down in the coffee shop at the bookstore.

After intensive scientific investigation (and several café lattés, with hazelnut flavoring and whipped cream), our researchers made the following breakthrough: Nutrition, it turns out, is just another word for *Chemistry!* That's right, seekers, it's all chemicals! And, since we at the Center For Adequate Living managed to avoid chemistry in high school (we opted for the life sciences course of study because it involved actual live animals, which we could name and take home at the end of the semester), this discovery came as quite a shock. Well, seekers, you will be as astonished as we were when you learn that nutritional guides are simply replete with such chemical terms as "Aspara Amino Benzoic Acid," "Inositol," "Pyridoxine," and "Potassium." These are terms that, let's face it, frighten the average adequate parent. Also, the authors warn us, these highly chemical substances must be combined with absolute precision in order to attain maximum nutritional value. Too much of one, too little of another, or the wrong combination will cause your children to become, at the very least, malnourished, attention-deficit, hyperactive, obese, chocoholic sociopaths.

Frankly, the whole subject just gave us major headaches (although, it may have been the café lattés). So, after self-medication (also, coincidentally, made up of chemicals), we began the task anew.

We are now ready to report our findings. Please take a moment to get a pencil and paper.

Dear seekers, after careful, completely

scientific, and frankly rather boring research, the
Center For Adequate Living will now divulge the
following advice on sufficiently fueling your children
so that they can become highly adequate, nearly
mature, and mostly well-adjusted adults. Our study
has revealed the following simple but highly scientific
nutritional guideline for the adequate parent. This is
the nutritional guideline that women's magazines
have not been able (or dared) to give you: Children
should eat. Food, whenever feasible. And in
quantities that satisfy their hunger. Parents would do
well to stay away from nutritional guides. Also, avoid
too many café lattés with hazelnut flavoring and
whipped cream. Remember our food motto . . .
Enough Good Food *Is* Enough Good Food. Have a
nutritionally adequate day.

# Parenting

*. . . we know many secrets as children, forget them as adults, and re-learn them through our children.*

$\mathcal{L}$ook at your spouse. Do you occasionally wonder just who that person is that you married? What happened to that sweet, loving, adorable person you've chosen as your life-mate? Are you becoming convinced that your spouse is not just a member of another sex, but another species? Do you often feel that the two of you are not just on a different page, but in a totally different book, written in two completely unrelated languages? Believe me, seekers, you are not alone! Chances are, your spouse feels the same way.

Many experts in the fields of psychology, sociology, and television talk shows have dedicated their lives to searching for the answers to the above questions, compiling and documenting their findings in literally thousands of self-help books, videos, tapes, etc., and then selling them to us. They all say the same thing. The reality is, men and women think, act and live quite differently together.

Gender differences are particularly notable in the area of parenting. We at the Center for Adequate Living are outstanding in the field of "Sexual Differences in the Different Sexes." Our extensive scientific studies have revealed that a large number of our subjects are members of opposing genders. Our research has shown that the most often cited marital conflicts are:

1. Money;
2. Sex;
3. Parenting.

Actually, parenting comes in second, if you combine money and sex, like most people do. Even I, adequate person that I am, occasionally find myself at odds with my own spouse, adequate spouse that he is, on how best to deal with our children, adequate though they are. We want to do the best for our children, but we just take opposite approaches. This can place great stress on a marriage, and, thus, upon the whole family. We at the Center For Adequate Living believe the following: The greatest gift you can give to your children is your own happy marriage. It is extremely important, therefore, for mothers and fathers to compromise and find a way to strike a balance in their parenting styles.

It was that great authority of painfully proper behavior, Lady Astor, who once said: "One does not *raise* children, one raises *chickens!* One *rears* children!" However, it has been our observation that, since the decline in popularity, and legality, of corporal punishment, we do not *rear* our children nearly as much as we used to!

But take heart, dear seekers, it *is* possible to send your children forth into this world as highly adequate, nearly mature, and mostly well-adjusted individuals. And, honestly, isn't that what we all desire for our children — for them to be able to find their niche, their own corner of the world — if possible, in another state? This is not an un-attainable goal, dear seekers! All it takes is patience, the above mentioned compromise, and the ability to get through life's conflicts — preferably without the use of controlled substances.

We believe that it is not that difficult to be an adequately functional family. Be attentive to the physical, emotional, as well as developmental needs of your children as they grow. Remember that example is far more effective than lecture (and far less boring). Cultivate your sense of humor, your ability to play, and your appreciation for the ridiculous. Keep your children safe and warm. Feed them well. Also, it's a good idea to have the locks changed when they move out.

We leave you, dear seekers, with the following touching offering. This poem was written by a young mother and it warmly and eloquently epitomizes the complex and often conflicting feelings that can exist between mothers and fathers:

It's not that we fight about how to raise kids
Our opinions are so close, it's eerie
It's just when it comes to day-to-day life
I'm practice . . . and he's mostly theory!

Hug your children (and your spouse) and have an adequate day.

# Dreams

*. . . dreams reveal our inner-most secrets.
Unfortunately we're unconscious at the time.*

$\mathcal{A}$dequacy seekers . . . did you have that
dream again last night — the one where you're driving
a runaway school bus with thirty terrified children,
careening down a mountain road heading straight for
a cliff?  And as you desperately try to gain control,
with the screams of the children filling the air, do you
suddenly realize that you're almost completely naked?
And just as the bus plunges over the cliff, with the
children shrieking, with you clutching the shreds of
clothing about your body, and with certain death
(and, even worse, humiliation) awaiting you on the

rocks below, do you suddenly wake up? Are you wondering what this dream may mean? Could it perhaps reflect an element of your current life situation — one that you'd better heed? Or, could it be that this nightmare portends dire events to come? Maybe you need to cut down on those midnight chocolate binges. What could be causing you to have such dreams?

We at the Center For Adequate Living are, as always, on the job! Not only are we able to ask you so many questions, we are going to answer them for you! We have just completed yet another in-depth scientific study. Fortunately for you, this particular research study was launched to determine the meaning of just such dreams as yours.

The dream state is mysterious. We do not understand the psychological and physiological changes in the brain that cause dreams. Our investigators spent many hours observing sleeping volunteers to determine just how the dream process works. What did we discover? For one thing we discovered that watching other people sleep is *incredibly boring*. In fact, it seems that the only dream research our people managed to conduct was on the dreams they had when they fell asleep during the research sessions. We were just about to give up on — I mean, conclude — this study some months ago when we suddenly stumbled upon an exciting scientific discovery! We still had grant money left! The deadline for our results, therefore, was extended.

We used the remainder of the grant funds to purchase a *Dictionary of Dreams*, a large supreme pizza, and several pitchers of beer, and spent a full evening intensively researching the meaning of your dream.

The book was quite clear on "automobile accident" dreams: "This common anxiety dream indicates the dreamer's feeling a lack of control over his or her life." Under "children" the book notes: "To dream of frightened children — especially if the dreamer is the cause of the fright, denotes trouble from the under-handed work of seemingly friendly people." Honestly, it actually says that! We at the Center For Adequate Living felt this was an especially funny interpretation. Particularly after the second pitcher of beer.

As for the "naked" part of your dream, our official guide informs us that: "To dream that you suddenly discover your nudity, and are trying to conceal it, denotes that you have sought illicit pleasure contrary to your noblest instincts and are anxious to conceal those desires." We at the Center For Adequate Living were, quite frankly, shocked and appalled!

After all the data had been carefully evaluated (*well* after last call), we concluded the following meanings for your dream: First of all, driving a runaway bus does *not* necessarily mean your life is out of control. Perhaps your subconscious is trying to tell you something else. Have you ever considered driving a school bus as a career choice? Nor do we feel that dreaming of endangering children means you should be wary of your friends (no more so than usual, anyway). What about going into child care? As for the nudity part, well, we suspect that our guide is right on the money. And we strongly suggest you seek intense, costly, and most likely agonizing psychotherapy immediately.

Clearly, this comprehensive scientific study has unraveled the mystery of your recurrent dream. We at the Center For Adequate Living are certain that these are absolutely rational and totally scientific interpretations. If you, or your attorneys, foolishly do not concur with our findings, or choose to criticize our methods, we would like to suggest that you *get your own damn grant!* And keep your clothes on!

# Driving

*. . . the secrets to safe driving include: hands on the wheel, eyes on the road, car in the garage.*

$\mathcal{A}$re you driving more and enjoying it less? Is it beginning to seem like every other driver around you is either drunk, on drugs, and/or psychotic? Is everyone in front of you an idiot? Is everyone behind you a maniac? Do you view other drivers as the enemy, sent by a malevolent force to provoke you into using your automobile as a weapon? We at the Center For Adequate Living feel that this is a very healthy attitude. Recently, the driving habits of our citizens have become so appalling that we decided to launch an emergency research project (even taking priority over our on-going study of reruns of *Quantum Leap*). We decided it was high time somebody took a close look at the behavior of people in their automobiles. Preferably from a safe distance.

We are happy to say our efforts were not totally wasted. We have discovered a little-understood but rapidly growing phenomenon among drivers. We refer to this auto-phenomenon as "Dwell." "Dwell" is based upon the premise that the average traffic light in the United States lasts approximately 60 seconds, while the attention span of the average American driver is approximately 54.5 seconds. Therefore, when the light changes, Mr. or Ms. Average, who is invariably in front of you, is no longer "there," so to speak, and does not move in a timely manner — or at all — sparking the previously mentioned deadly provocation. For reasons that are still unclear to our researchers, the "Dwell" phenomenon is quite often associated with — to put it technically — the digital exploration of inner nasal passages. Since the Center For Adequate Living is based in Indiana, we speak here of "Hoosier Dwell." In Ohio, one would refer to "Buckeye Dwell;" in the South it is known as "Dixie Dwell;" California has "Dude Dwell;" and in Washington, D.C. it is called "Congress."

Now, we do not propose that this knowledge alone will alleviate the frustrations that "Dwell" can cause. But, in the words of that great medical researcher Madame Marie Curie: "In order to cure a disease, you must first identify it." We believe we have identified an affliction that, if unchecked, will seriously affect the mental health and physical well-being of our entire nation. And we will not rest until we have researched, developed and implemented a workable solution. And we will begin this important work . . . right after *Quantum Leap.*

# Father's Day

*. . . the secret to being a good father — be honest, be fun-loving, be there.*

*O*h, remember the June of long ago? That lovely month in early summer with flowers in bloom, and warm fragrant evenings spent rocking on the porch, the silence unbroken except by crickets and children at play. And the only holiday one had to contemplate while rocking was a whole month away. In fact, at one time, June was one of only two months in the whole year blessedly free of holidays. June and August — two months with nothing to decorate, no presents to buy, no special foods to prepare or funny clothes to wear. That was, until 1910. In 1910, Mrs.

John Bruce Dodd of Seattle, Washington, apparently having little else to do — it being too early for soap operas by about forty years — decided that June was too quiet. She felt that the month needed some pizzazz, something to celebrate with her bridge and tea party crowd and maybe also to have an excuse to shoot off a few rounds of ammunition (not really, we just made that part up). So Mrs. Dodd decided to think up a holiday. She thought and thought and finally decided she would go out and buy her father a few useless gifts to take her mind off the problem. Right in the middle of the purchase of a particularly unattractive cravat, she suddenly shouted, "Eureka!" and was quietly escorted from the shop.

So in 1910, Father's Day was born. Well, technically, in 1924 — that's the year the government, in its infinite wisdom and glacier-like decisiveness, decided to go along with the gag and make it an official holiday.

The third Sunday in June is the day to pay homage to our fathers. Ah, Father! That man who made our lives so full, so rich, so . . . well, okay, not especially rich, nor actually that full, come to think of it. But he was the one who taught us how to ride that first two-wheeler (we still carry the scars), and put together our first "some-assembly-required" toys, where-upon we experienced our first colorful expletives. This was the man who frightened our very first boyfriends. And all the ones who came after until he frightened one so badly that the poor boy proposed. So don't we just owe that man some homage?

This is the day to think of our fathers fondly, shower them with gratitude, good deeds, and ridiculous gifts. We consistently and proudly wrap the wrong items — fishing tackle for fathers who don't fish, barbecue aprons for Dads who don't cook, golf tees for those who don't play golf, or, if they do, already have a million tees, and ties — literally millions of tasteless ties go directly from shops to garage sale tables every year because of this holiday. We simply have not been trained in appropriate gift selection for Father. Know why? We don't have a Father's Day Theme.

It seems that even the card and gift industries (who govern the rites and rituals of our holidays) are unsure of how to envision "Father." "Mother" is simple — her holiday theme is flowers. Christmas, Thanksgiving, Easter, Fourth of July, Halloween, and St. Patrick's Day all have their required and proper symbolic decorations, colors, cards, gifts, etc. Even Dr. Martin Luther King Jr.'s Birthday, Presidents' Day, and Memorial Day have their traditional observances and furniture sales.

Father's Day, though, seems to elude us. Let's explore this dilemma together. What says "Father"? And how can we best represent this in our purchases? We at the Center For Adequate Living have, coinciden-tally, recently completed a research study into this very subject. Our researchers in-vestigated a typical Cards 'N' Gifts 'N' $tuff establishment to scientifically determine the official "Father's Day Theme."

After careful scientific study, consisting of analyzing the artwork on hundreds of greeting cards and gift items, we have determined that there is, indeed a theme in our culture that says "masculine," "paternal," and even a little bit "frightening." That theme, oddly enough, dear seekers, is: duck hunting! Imagine! We found a plethora of duck decoys for the manly mantel, cards featuring pictures of faithful hounds clutching limp, dead fowl in their jaws, scenes of early mornings on cattail-infested waters, and other such duck-type items. It seems that every father in America (except possibly yours) hunts ducks. Occasionally quail, but mostly ducks. Yes, dear seekers, nothing says "Daddy" quite like a dead duck.

Now we can all go forth and meet Father's Day with confidence in our celebration and shopping abilities. Just remember — duck hunting!

We at the Center For Adequate Living, as
always, are proud and happy to have been of some
small assistance in yet another of life's quandaries.
And now we would like to offer a modest suggestion.
We feel that what this country needs is a National
Adequate Living Day.  We could celebrate it by
purchasing cards with adequate greetings, gifts of
adequate use, and just generally trying to feel
adequate all day.  What do you think?  August is kind
of quiet . . . Have a Happy Adequate Living Day.

# Holiday Planning

*. . . a time frought with secret expectations, anxieties, hopes, and pure stress — dreaded and desired at the same time. A small suggestion . . .*

Imagine this. It's Christmas Eve, and Mom and Dad are by the fire, smiling lovingly at each other and sipping eggnog. Under the magnificent tree are the gifts, bought and beautifully wrapped weeks before Thanksgiving, and hidden safely in Mom's closet. Upstairs, the children are happily helping each other wrap the presents they bought with their own money. The aroma of Grandma's ginger cookies mingles with the pine scent of the tree. Grandpa is just putting the finishing touches on a handmade doll house. Outside it is snowing, and the sound of caroling drifts through the air. The carolers are invited in for holiday cheer. The family and the neighborhood singers share eggnog and warm cookies by the fire. Everyone is relaxed. Everyone is happy. This is the best Christmas ever! Where are we? Well, most likely we're in a greeting card commercial, because no real family has had a Christmas like that — *ever*!

Let us now consider the reality of Christmas Eve in the adequate household:

Dad is on a frantic last-minute shopping spree at the corner drug store, trying to find tinsel and tree lights because the ones at home are such a tangled mess that the only way they would go onto the tree is in one large lump. Next we find him in the cosmetic department trying to decide between the gallon jug of purple bubble bath or the quart bottle of generic "White Shoulders" perfume as a gift for Mom. Apparently, he is unaware that Mom is allergic to bubble bath and hasn't worn "White Shoulders" since junior high school. He then hits the toy department to snap up the last bag of toy soldiers for his boy and cartoon coloring book for the baby, even though his boy is now eighteen and the baby just got her driver's license.

Mom is in a frenzy, searching for the gifts that she's hidden too well. She is shocked when she opens a drawer and discovers the 157 Christmas cards, addressed, stamped and sealed (including the annual two-page "family update letter" that she spent two weeks composing). Her son sort of forgot to mail them. Upstairs the children are fighting over who gets to give Mom the same vase they bought her last year. Grandma's burning ginger cookies set off the smoke alarm and everyone heads outside until the fire department gives the all-clear. Carolers wander by, Mom invites them in for some holiday cheer, which turns out to be cheese doodles and grape soda because the cookies are ruined and Grandpa made off with the eggnog. Once inside, the carolers inform Mom that they also sell a unique line of cleaning products and proceed to pour the soda onto the carpet for a demonstration. Dad arrives with his packages, sees the mess, and suddenly loses his tenuous grasp of the holiday spirit along with his temper. Everyone is anxious. Everyone is stressed. This is not the best Christmas. But it's certainly more typical than our first scenario.

Dear adequacy seekers, do you find yourself facing Christmas with a mixture of emotions, made up of anticipation, hope, confidence, apprehension, anxiety, dread, and a large amount of pure stoicism? Media messages remind us that it's our solemn duty to make this holiday season perfect. And, as always,

our media mentors demand: "Have Your Best
Holidays Ever!" "Make this Your Family's Most
Memorable Christmas!" and "Be Perfect this Season —
Or Else!"  Okay, we made up that last one.  But the
expectation is there.  If we just follow their plans,
time lines, decorating ideas, gift and baking tips, then
we, too, should have a perfect holiday season.  It's
simply up to us.

      We at the Center For Adequate Living know
better.  In order for us to create the perfect holiday,
we must first navigate a treacherous mine field
consisting of grouchy spouses, uncooperative
children, demanding relatives, emotionally unstable
friends, muddy dogs, and churlish cats.  And that's
just at home.  We also must face stressed-out bosses,
irritable co-workers, harrowing traffic, and surly
salespeople.  When our noblest aspirations collide
with these real-life obstacles, the results are, alas,
predictable.

      Each year, it seems that we begin this season
with high hopes and reach New Year's Day with, at
the very least, a vague sense of disappointment and,
at worst, a full-blown case of self-pity and depression.
We wonder why we do this to ourselves.  And yet, we
know that we will do it again.  Once again we will set
our expectations up on the highest bough.  We grit
our teeth, deck the halls, and strive to make merry.

If only we didn't strive quite so hard. Wouldn't it be wonderful if we simply, just this once, *did not* attempt perfection for a change? Most of us do not realize this, but, we actually have the power — and the right — to change the rules. Yes, we have. Imagine, we can escape the tradition traps. Blasphemy? Perhaps. But consider the possibility for yourself for just a moment. Let's say, for example, that you exhaust yourself making cinnamon bread every year for all of your family and friends. It has become a tradition, an expectation among your loved ones. And every year, there seem to be more and more loved ones with the expectation of fresh, fragrant bread from you. Suppose this year you buy bakery bread for your family and give gift certificates for loaves to all of the others. And when they look at you quizzically, suppose you simply smile. And let's say you approach all of your holiday planning with that attitude. Instead of the two-page "Christmas Greeting Letter" that you must create every year, suppose you simply leave it out. Or, perhaps, write one line: "All hell has broken loose, call for details." Just think of the folks you'd hear from! Afraid you'll disappoint people? Well, you might. Possibly. For a short moment. Just keep smiling. Maybe this could be the year your children remember as being "the year Mommy and Daddy weren't tired and grouchy all the time." Maybe you'll reach New Year's Day with a little more energy and a little more optimism. Hey, no pressure. It's just a thought.

Keep in mind our motto: Good Enough *Is* Good Enough. Take a deep breath and have an adequate holiday season, however you choose to celebrate.

# Mid-Life

*. . . the secret to staying young: eat healthy, keep fit, lie about your age.*

$\mathcal{D}$ear adequacy seekers . . . have you noticed anything strange when you look in the mirror? Is there someone else looking back — resembling one of your parents, maybe? Or, possibly that aunt you never really liked but everyone said you'd look just like her one day and *there she is?* As those of you who have spent any time in a grocery line lately must know by now, our beloved "Baby Boom" generation is sliding inexorably and frantically into what is called "Mid-Life." The first official post-World War II baby turned fifty in May of 1996 (How we came up with that date: Japan surrendered on Aug. 15, 1945, therefore the first post-war-conceived baby would have been born in May, 1946. But you knew that), and an entire demo-graphic category has been in crisis ever since. We at the Center For Adequate Living have been watching this phenomenon with great interest because, after all, we are responsible for keeping our finger upon the pulse of the Adequate American and we are, quite frankly, disturbed by a quickening of that pulse among those approaching this euphemistically labeled "Mid-Life."

First of all, the term "Mid-Life" is certainly a misnomer. Fifty can only be considered "Mid-Life" if one lives to be one hundred. Secondly, these Baby-Boomers are the ones who founded the Youth Move-ment, a generation obsessed with youth, physical perfection, and sexual prowess. They have, in effect, created a culture in which they, themselves, are becoming obsolete. They are the ones who were never going to be thirty; and they never will . . . again. So we at the Center For Adequate Living have launched a study into Mid-Life — specifically: 1. What is it? 2. What can be done about it? 3. How can we at the Center For Adequate Living make money from it?

1. What, exactly, is Mid-Life and how can you tell if you are a potential casualty? Consider the following indications. Mid-Life is a time when you:
- no longer hope a ringing telephone is for you;
- don't look forward to getting the mail;

- have finally, *finally* admitted that no matter how hard you train, no matter how many hours you put into it, you will probably never play center field for the Yankees, or dance with the New York Ballet Company;
- discover that your broad mind and narrow waist have changed places;
- are certain that you can never again pursue buns-, thighs-, abs-, nor any other body parts-of-steel because of your iron-poor blood;
- find yourself thinking, "Grandma Moses didn't start painting until she was in her 80s," and take comfort in that thought;
- begin to suspect that, after all those years of pretending not to care what the world thinks of you, it seems the world wasn't even watching;
- never wear anything that could remotely be described as "kicky;"
- don't trust anyone *under* the age of thirty;
- purposely choose comfort over fashion.

    2. Now that we have determined your eligibility into this not-so-exclusive club, we have one question: *Must* you crisis? Dear seekers, we beg you to consider the following scientific fact: *People get older.* It's inevitable, inescapable, and — here's the important thing — it's part of the growing process. Honestly! That's why it's called "*growing* older." The

alternative to growing older is to stop growing altogether, which means to *die* altogether. Therefore, the only scientifically proven method of staying young is to die. We at the Center For Adequate Living do not recommend this method.

We do suggest, however, that you seriously consider adjusting your attitude about growing older, emphasize the *growing* instead of the *older*. That icon to growing old gracefully, the cosmetically inclined Elizabeth Arden, once said, "People who are concerned with age are silly, you're only as old as you feel!" Our question for Ms. Arden is: "As you feel to whom?" But that's beside the point. She's right, of course. Attitude is everything. Always keep in mind, our goal is adequacy, not perfection. So if you find you'd rather watch reruns of *Quantum Leap* than speed-walk five miles (and who wouldn't?), go easy on yourself! And, believe it or not, *one* Snickers bar never made anyone fat.

Go look in a mirror. Go right now. Look your-self in the eye and repeat: "I'm adequate, I'm highly adequate." Repeat this phrase until you can no longer say it with a straight face. Then get out there and go on with your life. Because if you don't . . . it *will* go on without you.

Have an adequate Mid-Life. That'll be $10 (3).

# Total Fitness System

*. . . the secrets to staying fit and healthy are not between the covers of a book or the pages of a magazine, but between our own ears.*

*W*ell, here you are, once again at that time of year when you begin to seriously consider getting into shape. Yes, we are aware that your New Year's resolution to lose weight and exercise hit the skids by mid-January. And we know that between the lousy weather and the abundance of Valentine chocolates, your will power has been simply devastated. It's not your fault. Your busy career and active social schedule leaves you precious little time to even contemplate your physical fitness needs. Often, it seems society itself is determined to undermine your resolve. Everywhere you look are mixed messages ("Lose 10 Pounds by Spring - page 30" and "Luscious Desserts to Die For - page 31"). And yet you know that fitness is exactly what you need to help you keep up with your exciting social schedule and incredibly rewarding career. What can you do? To whom can you turn? Jane Fonda? Not anymore. She's now married to bazillionaire Ted Turner and no longer cares what happens to us common folk. Kathy Smith? Heavens no, she's obviously never had a weight problem in her life and is so beautiful, her videos produce more depression than fitness. Richard Simmons? Not unless being completely annoyed burns a lot of calories. Susan Powter? *Puleeeeeeze.* No, dear seekers, none of them can give you what you need — a *personal* touch, sensitive to your unique lifestyle, adjusted to your daily routine. Who can help you? Who can provide this vital assistance for you? Why, the Center For Adequate Living, silly!

You will be gratified to know that we at the Center For Adequate Living have been working day and night — sadly neglecting our own fitness needs — to develop the following daily diet and exercise system. This system can be easily incorporated into your own already full (and fulfilling) day. We have even included self-talk suggestions that will help keep you motivated! All without taking any time away from your own dazzling career and scintillating social schedule.  We call this:

## THE TOTAL FITNESS SYSTEM FOR THE ADEQUATE LIFESTYLE

**5:00 AM:** 30-minute run, 30-minute weight training, 30-minute yoga-stretch cool-down, brisk 10-minute cool shower.  Sip one cup hot water with lemon while preparing power breakfast and packing nutritious lunch.

**SELF-TALK:** "Today *will* be a successful, healthful day."

**BREAKFAST:** 1/2 grapefruit sprinkled with 1 tbsp. raw wheat germ, one piece whole wheat toast, dry, 8 oz. skim milk.

**SELF-TALK:** "Today I will park at least 1/2 mile away from office and walk briskly to work. Invigorating!"

**10:00 AM:** One small orange, 16 oz. bottled water.

**SELF-TALK:** "5 minutes of deep breathing instead of coffee at break will stimulate creative thinking!"

**LUNCH:** 4 oz. lean broiled chicken, mixed green salad, no dressing, 16 oz. bottled water, one cookie, one cup herbal tea.

**SELF-TALK:** "Spending a portion of lunch break doing stomach crunches in the lady's room helps start the afternoon off right!"

**2:00 PM:** The rest of the package of cookies.

**SELF-TALK:** "Well, they would have just gone to waste! Besides, I'm sure those women from the secretarial pool were gossiping about me in the lunchroom again and *they're* certainly not getting any of *my* cookies! I'll just do a few more minutes of exercise tomorrow."

**4:00 PM:** three cups coffee, with real sugar and cream, two Snickers bars.

**SELF-TALK:** "After that horrible meeting with my boss, I deserve it!"

**5:00 PM:** Take taxi to car. Share large bag of barbecue chips with driver.

**SELF-TALK:** "This is a bad neighborhood! What was I *thinking* parking that far away? It's just inviting disaster! At least I didn't eat the whole bag myself!"

**DINNER:** One large supreme pizza, one six pack beer, not light, one quart chocolate-chocolate chip ice cream, whipped cream and pecans.

**SELF-TALK:** "Men are all jerks! Why in the world did I ever go out with that guy? The least he can do is call! Who can blame me if I need some comfort food?"

**11:00 PM:** Entire cheesecake eaten directly from the freezer.

**SELF-TALK:** "Shut up!"

Ah, dear seekers, do remember — tomorrow is another day! Forgive yourself and have an adequate day.

# Envy

*. . . the secret here is that it is not just virtuous to welcome the good fortune of others, it is essential to our own good fortune.*

$\mathcal{D}$o you have that uneasy feeling again?  That feeling that someone is out-performing, out-earning, out-*lifestyling* you?  Do you find yourself suffering from that dreadful and highly deadly sin — caught once again in the power of the green-eyed monster — *ENVY*?  Do you gaze wistfully at others, coveting their cool demeanor, their seemingly endless energy, organizational skills, and obvious control over their lives?  Does this cause you to feel — dare I say — *inadequate* by comparison?  We at the Center For Adequate Living strongly suggest you *snap out of it!* Your current mood, if left unchecked, will certainly take a turn for the worse and become that eighth and deadliest of sins — SELF-PITY. Even we, adequate though we are, occasionally fall into the pit of this destructive emotion. Self-pity, envy, regret, and guilt are the quadruplets of sorrow; the four horsemen of wasted energy and useless suffering; the unbelievably appropriate metaphor of distress.

Now, take a good look around you. Upon closer observation, you will find that things are not what they seem. It is a fact that the very people you envy are in no more control of their lives than you are of yours. Oh, certainly, that young executive down the hall looks as if she has it all together. She's dressed in the latest corporate fashion; her shoes match — each other; she's got a picture of her perfect children on her infuriatingly clutter-free desk; she has a personalized, leather-bound date book that she consults frequently; and she carries a designer workout bag.

But the truth is, dear seeker, your observations simply do not correspond with the facts. Beneath that cool facade (you will be delighted to know) she's every bit as frantic as you are! She's praying that no one notices that she's worn the same suit three times this week because she can't remember which cleaners she took the rest of her clothes to. Those shoes she's wearing are the only pair her children didn't sell in their little garage sale (the babysitter didn't think she'd mind!). Her desk became clean during a desperate attempt to find the highly confidential market report she worked on day and night for three weeks (only to discover that her daughter took thirty copies of it to school for show-and-tell). And that is not a picture of her children — it came with the frame and she can't find the time to get a photo of her own kids that fits it. The personalized, leather-bound cover is not a date book at all, it's covering a romance novel that she reads in meetings while pretending to consult her schedule. Also, she doesn't really work out. She's been carrying around her son's dirty gym clothes and her own uneaten lunch in that Gucci bag for several weeks. She's afraid to open it.

She's juggling five things at once, three of which are on fire. Just like you. And just like all of us, in her life, there are too many pies and too few fingers. She too, in the words of that great philosopher/song writer/curmudgeon Tom Lehrer, is "sliding down the razor blade of life." Let's face it, she's not doing very well at all. Now, doesn't that make you feel better?

So, dear seekers, don't allow envy to ruin an otherwise perfectly adequate day. As we have shown, things are not always as they appear. Besides, haven't you noticed the envious way she's been looking at you?

# Mr. Right

*. . . the secret to a good marriage is finding someone who has those attributes we admire but do not possess, and then resisting the urge to promptly change them.*

$\mathcal{A}$dequacy seekers . . . Are you unhappily single? Have you been searching for your Mr. Right, Mr. Perfect, but lately you'd seriously consider Mr. Not-So-Bad-Considering?  When you meet a man who, at first glance, appears to be exactly right for you, do you wish there was some way to scientifically test your compatibility?,  A concise, quantitative method to determine if he is *the one for you? Is* there such a method?  Well, of course there is!  And we at the Center For Adequate Living, as always, can provide it.

After thorough research consisting of examining advice given in various women's magazines, psychic help lines, and day-time talk shows, we now have conclusive scientific evidence proving that day-time talk shows cause insanity. No, sorry, that was a different study.

We did discover, though, that many women's publications tend to address important life situations through the "Quiz" method ("Are You Assertive Enough? Take This Quiz and See!", "Are You Happy? Take This Quiz and See!", "Do You Have a Fatal Disease? Take This Quiz and See!"). And since these publications seem to be making millions, who are we to disapprove? *Au contraire*, in their spirit of providing-scant-useful-information-while-being-moderately-entertaining-and-generally-hoping-to-rake-in-large-profits, we are jumping right on the "Quiz" bandwagon. Here, then, is the precise procedure to determine your future happiness:

### IS HE MR. RIGHT?  TAKE THIS QUIZ AND SEE!

The answers to the following questions will determine whether your alleged beloved is an adequate potential partner for you. Complete the following sentences by choosing A), B), or C):

1. **You're expecting him for an elegant evening. He arrives with:**

   **A)** flowers, a bottle of fine wine, and a limousine

**B)** three friends, four pizzas and a case of beer because, after all, it *is* the playoffs

**C)** a date

2. **You've had your first disagreement. You have agonized all day about it and decided to have a heart-to-heart talk with him. He says:**

**A)** "Yes, I am also concerned and would like to discuss where our relationship is going."

**B)** "I was wrong, you were right. Got any beer?"

**C)** Nothing. Not only does he not remember having an argument, he's having trouble with your name

3. **He tells you he was trained for his profession:**

**A)** at Harvard — but he modestly explains that he was only second in his class

**B)** by his father, who will bring him into the business, if you would just co-sign a loan

**C)** well, he only has to complete a couple of classes, but life's too short to worry about the future

4. **He lets you know that there will be no problem with former girlfriends because:**

**A)** your relationship is so special, it's as if he had no others

**B)** his former girlfriends cross the street when they see him coming

**C)** numerous restraining orders are in force

5. **You find yourself humming "The Wedding March." He finds himself breaking into:**

**A)** "Some Enchanted Evening"

**B)** "My Baby Does the Hanky Panky"

**C)** hives

6. **He thinks the ideal furniture for your place should be:**

**A)** elegant, in your color scheme, and from the very finest stores

**B)** from a discount store, on sale, and bought the day you need it

**C)** borrowed from his parents, when they're not home

7. **He doesn't pick up his dirty clothes from the floor. When you mention it to him, he says:**

**A)** "I'm so sorry, darling, I guess I'll need to change my ways in that department! It won't happen again."

**B)** "How else can I find them when I want to wear them again?"

**C)** "What clothes?"

8. **You are having dinner at an expensive restaurant. He lifts his glass, looks into your eyes and says:**

**A)** "To the most beautiful girl in the place. You take my breath away!"

**B)** "Is that a bug in my drink?"

**C)** (to the waiter) "Send one of these over to that girl at the bar."

9. **You're at an island resort, on the beach, at sunset. The soft sounds of the ocean are all you hear. He has a far-off, wistful look on his face. Suddenly he turns to you and says:**

**A)** "This is wonderful. I want it to last forever. Will you marry me?"

**B)** "This is wonderful. Are you going to finish that piña colada?"

**C)** "This is wonderful. So, do they get ESPN at this hotel?"

The scoring of this quiz should be evident. If you chose mostly:

**A)s** Marry him. But first we suggest you have the prescription checked on those rose-colored glasses, and buy yourself some "Disappointment" Insurance.

**B)s** Marry him. And do so with the knowledge that you have a strong grasp on reality and a keen sense of "guy" thinking. You poor thing.

**C)s** Marry him. This guy is just waiting for the right woman to come along to help him become the best he can be. He'll be your ultimate refinishing project!

Surely you didn't think we would give you any other advice! Don't be silly! It is totally consistent with our motto. You *do* remember our motto: Good Enough *Is* Good Enough. Have an adequate marriage.

# Encouragement for a Difficult Day

*. . . the secret to getting through any difficulty is to
remember the four most powerful words in the English
language: "This too shall pass." And to find
a bit of perspective.*

*A*dequacy seekers . . . Are you finding it difficult
to get through the problem-filled, angst-ridden, un-
relenting work-a-day drudgery that you call your life?
Do you long to break free, to lessen your burdens, heal
your soul?  We at the Center For Adequate Living have
the following encouraging words for you:
*Go to Cleveland.*

You will be amazed to discover that there are
hundreds of thousands of people in Cleveland who have
never heard of you or your petty problems.  They don't
know your name, or the name of anyone you know.  And

what's even better, they don't care! Isn't that great? We have found that this scientific method of self-healing works even if you *live* in Cleveland. You can then return to your own insignificant little life with a renewed sense of perspective and the comforting knowledge that, indeed, you truly *are* alone in this world! Now, doesn't that make you feel much better?

Remember our motto: Good Enough *Is* Good Enough. Have an adequate day.

# Theme Parks

*. . . life is a lot like a theme park, noisy, crowded, and filled with oddly dressed characters.*

$\mathcal{A}$re you ready for a break? Need to escape? Is it family vacation time? Not sure what to do, where to go? Well, you are in luck, because The Center For Adequate Living has just completed a study of one of the most popular vacation destinations — the Theme Park. And as soon as we recover, we will share our results with you.

At the risk of being struck by lightning, as well as unpleasant and possibly litigious mail, we have concluded the following: *A Theme Park is no place for small children!* "What!" some will cry, "Theme Parks were created *just* for children, designed so that their angelic faces will light up when the Copyrighted

Cartoon Characters meet them right at the gate to personally guide them through a day (or several days, depending upon the package) of delight, joy, and also rapture! How can *anyone* find fault with that?" To those folks we say, Bah! And also Humbug! In fact, we firmly believe that no one under the age of — at least — eight should even be *allowed* into a Theme Park. Now, we know some others who might say, "I took my two-year-old triplets and had a great time!" and we suppose that is possible. But it would be, statistically speaking, the tail end of a normal distribution. In other words, we don't believe it.

The fact is that huge amusement parks are bewildering conglomerations of overstimulating, frustrating, and often downright frightening experiences for a tender young psyche. This is the psychological equivalent to putting the newest, most colorful, and heavily advertised toy in front of a child and then saying that she cannot touch it for up to two hours. Meanwhile, she must watch hundreds of other children play with it. Most children do not take kindly to such restriction. And yet, this is exactly what parents do when they get in line for "Mr. Copyrighted Cartoon Character's Big Thrilling Ride" and expect kids to wait hours for a two minute thrill (which, by the time it happens, often becomes two minutes of terror followed by "Again!"). We observed some quite appalling parental behavior caused by the simple fact that *no one* can happily wind through cattle chutes behind thousands of other bodies for a couple of hours to get to *anything.* And when children are bored/frustrated/tired, they tend to behave like, well, bored/frustrated/tired children. Many parents seemed surprised and angered by this (to us) totally appropriate behavior.

**NOTE TO THE PENTAGON**: Looking for the perfect fighting force? When battle breaks out in some foreign hot spot, just drop in a battalion of mothers who have been in line for hours with three antsy kids and tell them that the enemy has just attempted to break into line in front of them. Hell hath no fury!

Now, let's consider this trip for older children. We admit it, Theme Parks are fun! As noted above, however, a large amount of time is spent standing in line. Our study shows that what separates a highly adequate Theme Park experience from a highly disagreeable one is the ability to have fun *while standing in line.* Once at the front of the line, the Theme Parks provide the fun, so we will forgo the typical "which ride to dash to" recommendation. Instead, we will provide you with the following list of items you will need in order to make the most of your "in line" time:

1. Bubbles. They are always fun and can entertain others around you;
2. Logic games, word puzzles, anything that takes thinking and time;
3. Several retractable fabric store measuring tapes. Not just for your kids, but also for the restless ones around you. Babies are mesmerized pulling the tape and pushing the button, older kids will run around measuring stuff. Just ask the parents' permission before offering;
4. A set of juggling balls. By the end of the day, you will be an expert — at laughing at yourself;
5. A book of jokes, riddles, anything humorous that can be read in short spurts;
6. Your sense of humor. Absolutely essential.

Come to think of it, these are all things you should have with you *at all times*. Because, if we may wax philosophical here, life is a lot like a Theme Park, isn't it? A lot of time is spent waiting for the thrills, which are pretty far apart and much too short; we're surrounded by others who are waiting in various stages of anticipation and frustration; no matter how early we start or how fast we go, we can never get it all in; and the whole thing costs much more than we expected. And, in the end, the difference between having a highly adequate life and a highly disagreeable one is the ability to *have fun while waiting!* Think about it and have an adequate family vacation.

# The Soaps

*. . . all of the secrets of successful living are found in day-time drama — money, makeup, lavish digs, and an evil twin or two.*

Because you are so very busy leading your extremely important, highly productive, and incredibly fulfilling life (and because it's our bet you have not yet figured out how to set the timer on your video tape machine), we know it is difficult for you to keep up with your favorite day-time dramas.  Therefore, we have, for purely altruistic reasons and at quite a considerable inconvenience, spent the entire week watching these shows, taking notes, so we can provide you with the following valuable service. Below are synopses of some of the most popular "stories" on the air today:

## ALL MY CHILDREN ARE FROM ANOTHER WORLD

Fesuvial was stunned when he discovered inadvertently that he was the father of Rosinda's illegitimate child, Persius, particularly since he'd never slept with her. Ralph and Diana exchanged a significant look. Dolf became enraged with Chandra when she threatened to mess up his hair. His attempt to storm out of their luxurious penthouse apartment was foiled once again by the foyer mirror, which he could never quite get past. He spent the next six hours on a particularly stubborn cowlick. Drusilla suddenly died under mysterious circumstances.

## GET A LIFE TO LIVE

Mackenzie insisted to Lief that she never meant to reveal to Irving that he had been secretly married to Narissa while he was still married to Xenia and that he was the father of Spring's illegitimate child, Zeus. Mackenzie and Irving exchanged significant looks, twice. A mysterious woman appeared suddenly in Humbert's upscale condo, telling Irving her name was Drusilla and she was actually Humbert's long-lost daughter who had been suffering from amnesia and suddenly remembered she was heiress to Humbert's enormous estate. Irving developed an uncontrollable tick and admitted himself for psychiatric evaluation (send your cards and letters to "Our Lady of the Severely Confused"). Cody suddenly died under mysterious circumstances.

## THE YOUNG AND THE WRESTLERS

Joy was inconsolable when she inadvertently learned that her name actually means "joy." Brett's innocent remark to Melvin about a "full nelson" brought unfortunate results. A mystery man, Cody — a dead ringer for Trent who died mysteriously during last season's contract negotiations — appeared at Trista's lavish island estate explaining that he was Trent's long-lost twin brother who was kidnapped at birth and forced to become an accountant in Newark. Noreen had an illegitimate child, Poseidon, refusing to reveal the father's name. Kyle, Fritz, Rod, and the entire monastery, after exchanging significant looks, split the cost of a billboard that said simply, "It Wasn't Me!" Tiffany suddenly died under mysterious circumstances.

## LOSING

Christopher was astonished to discover that he had won Mira from Johnny Jack in a staring contest. Shortly after, Sonja informed Johnny Jack that Christopher is blind. Holly revealed to her father, Cecil, that, after she gives birth to the illegitimate child she conceived while being held hostage by aliens, she plans to enroll in the prestigious Graduate School of Aerobics at State U. Cecil immediately attempted suicide (please don't send any cards or letters, folks, this is *make-believe!*). Many significant looks were exchanged, except by Christopher. A mysterious stranger,

Tiffany, suddenly arrived at Christopher's opulent mountain cottage, claiming to be his long-lost wife who, for two seasons, was under the spell of her alter ego, Bruce, and lived at Muscle Beach with a Merchant Marine named Bo-Bo. Christopher didn't notice her presence. Mira stormed out into a blizzard, fell off a cliff, and died mysteriously. Christopher didn't notice her absence.

## TERMINAL HOSPITAL

Alphonso could not control his rage when the new nurse, Monica, suggested he visit a patient outside of "rounds." In his anger, he filled out all of the "special offering" cards from every magazine in the waiting room with her name and address. Monica began receiving dolls, plates, and figurines daily, each with its own "letter of authenticity." Frantic, Monica appealed to Drew, which was odd because he had never noticed her before. Nevertheless, Drew had her committed. In Operating Room 12, Steven, Rory, Brooke, and Hannah prepared to perform a delicate hamstring operation on Achilles, unaware that he was actually Steven and Brooke's illegitimate child. They were surprised to be introduced to the mysterious new anesthesiologist, Mira, who claimed to be their long-lost anesthesiologist who was accidentally frozen in the hospital's secret cryogenics lab ten years earlier and then accidentally thawed out when the custodian left a window open. They were all so busy exchanging significant looks that the patient mysteriously died.

Dear seekers, we at the Center For Adequate Living hope our efforts to keep you informed and up-to-date have been successful. Unfortunately, we have fallen woefully behind in our ongoing research of reruns of *Quantum Leap.* We will now go back to it. Have an adequately dramatic day.

# Other Thoughts

# The Ticket

*My* husband told me it was going to happen. That *very morning*, he warned me. I didn't believe him. But he is an excellent prognosticator — in the twenty-five years we've been together, I should have learned this. He warned me to replace my stolen driver's license. He said I'd get pulled over and be in big trouble. I scoffed. I've been driving for over thirty years now and have never been stopped. A pretty decent record, if you ask me. Oh, well, there *was* that one tiny citation for turning left at a "No-Left-Turn-After-4:00" trap downtown, but it was — I swear — 4:02! Other than that — and that was twenty years ago — I've been a card-carrying safe driver. Until yesterday. I was pulled over for speeding yesterday.

63

He was a motorcycle policeman.  Enormous
Harley Davidson, black leather jacket, boots, and
gloves, helmet, mirrored sunglasses, night stick,
scowl, *gun*.  He had stepped into the street, pointed
angrily at me and motioned toward the curb.  As I
pulled over (across two lanes — empty, thank
heavens, for I didn't exactly look), my daughter
became anxious.  "Are we going to get arrested?"  "No,
honey, he's only going to give me a ticket."  Only.  I
cursed myself for not paying attention, for my
procrastination in replacing my license, for getting
caught, and my husband for being so right!  I was not
going to hear the end of this one.  My run of luck was
over.

He approached the car warily, sidling up from
the back like they do on TV.  Although it seems that a
bright red mini-van with a woman and a little girl
inside would not pose much of a threat, one can never
be too careful, I suppose.

"Are you aware you were doing 47 in a 30 zone,
Ma'am?"  Evidently not.  "I was just keeping up with
the traffic . . ." I began lamely.  "Well, Ma'am," he
snarled, "you're the one we clocked — 47 in a 30.
May I see your license and registration, please?"  Very
polite, very intimidating.

I gave him what I hoped was a charming smile.
"I don't have a license at the moment."  "At the

moment, Ma'am?" I watched an eyebrow rise above the sunglasses. "Well, you see, my purse was stolen and I haven't replaced my license yet." Meanwhile, I fumbled through the pile of papers from the glove compartment hoping to recognize the registration.

Emily tried to help. "Cool sunglasses," she offered. "I beg your pardon?" He leaned in to hear her. "Cool sunglasses," she repeated. He smiled slightly. "Thanks." "Figures!" I mumbled as I sifted through receipts, lists, gum wrappers, junk. "The first time I get stopped *would be* the only time I don't have my license!" "Oh no, Mom," Emily said eagerly, "this isn't the first time! Remember that time you . . ." A stern look silenced her. I heard a chuckle from the officer. He asked my name, address, and other information from my missing license. When we got to my weight I said, "One hundred twenty . . . five," "Too late," he said smiling. "I already wrote 120." "Great! Now you can add perjury to my crimes." He continued smiling, and continued writing.

Emily was determined to help. "You're nicer than most policemen!" she declared. I looked at her. "How do you know what most policemen are like? You haven't been around that many." "Oh sure I have! Lots of times with Daddy!" Now the officer was laughing out loud. My head lowered to the steering wheel. "Emily," I said through clenched teeth, "you have the right to remain silent. May I suggest you exercise that right NOW!" Snickering, the now amiable policeman said, "Tell you what, Ma'am, I'm going to put the speeding citation into my warning file. I'll still have to cite you for not having a license in your possession. I suggest you replace it as soon as possible." He began writing out a new form. Noticing the time, Emily bemoaned the fact that she would now be late for school. "I was *trying* to get you there on time!" I cried. Ungrateful child! "Well, Ma'am," the officer said, "now you won't have to worry, 'cause you're *gonna* be late. And next time, don't try so hard."

Handing me the ticket, he pointed to the procedure for contesting the citation on the back and explained that I could go to court if I wanted. "Why would I want to do that? I'm guilty." "A lot of guilty people contest, Ma'am," he explained, moving away from the car. I stuck my head out of the window. "Successfully?" I inquired to his back. He straddled his bike and buckled up his helmet, shaking his head and laughing.

Continuing on our way, I attempted to admonish my daughter about being too flip with authority figures. As a beautiful, engaging child, she can get away with it (not to mention the fact that she saved me a moving violation), but as she gets older,

she may find officers of the law less inclined to a
sense of humor and one must learn discretion. "You
don't know it, Mom," she said proudly, "but I was
using a lot of discretion! Daddy told me what to say
to a policeman if I'm ever with him when *he's*
stopped!" I hesitated, afraid to ask. "OK, I'll bite.
What did Daddy tell you to say?" "I'm supposed to
say: 'Whatsamatta officer, Dunkin' Donuts closed?'"
I drove on, counting my blessings and watching my
speed.

# The Simple Life

*The* idea came to me on vacation. We had rented a condominium that had all the comforts of home. I loved the simplicity of the place. Especially the kitchen. There was one of everything we needed. We used it, washed it, and put it back. A place for everything and everything in its place. This was so unlike my home kitchen, cluttered with twenty-one years of marriage stuff and fourteen years of kid stuff. When I got home, I vowed, I would simplify, unclutter, and organize my kitchen. My mind filled with the possibilities. Perhaps then I could actually finish a thirty-minute dinner in thirty minutes. I could answer my husband's "Honey, where is the . . ." with confidence, and without having to get up. I would — dare I say it — *be in control of my kitchen again!* I would be a paragon of the simple life. This was my quest.

I opened a cabinet to begin the daunting task. An array of mostly familiar kitchen items was displayed before me, bowls of many sizes and materials, baking pans of various ages and conditions, and a stack of margarine tubs with no lids. I narrowed my eyes. Best to just take everything out and put back only what I really used. With a trash bag and a "charity" box at hand, I dug in. If an item was useful but had not been used in the past six months, it went into the box. Anything broken, cracked, warped, or unidentifiable was to be tossed. A cluttered house is a sign of a cluttered life. Out went the margarine tubs, warped cookie sheets, and dog-chewed bowls. No mercy! I was a lean, mean, cleaning machine. This was going to be simple!

My ten-year-old wandered in. She pulled something from the box. "Mom, you weren't going to get rid of this were you?" I looked at the item in question — a peculiar drinking glass with fish, sparkles, and The Little Mermaid floating between two layers of plastic. "You can't throw this out, it's my shot glass!" "I beg your pardon? Your what?" I thought perhaps I hadn't heard her correctly. "You know," she said, "When we were in Florida that time and I got sick and you took me to that awful doctor who gave me that horrible shot and you had to hold me down? Remember? This is

the glass Daddy bought me at Disney World to make
me feel better.  It's my shot glass.  I have to keep it!"
Hmmm.  The glass went back into the cabinet.

Reaching back, I knocked over a small cut-glass
"vinegar cruet" that my mother had given me.  A silly
gift.  Who needs a container just for vinegar?  I tried
putting salad dressing in it once, but the opening was
too small and it got stopped up.  So I had just stuck it
in the back of the cabinet, thinking I would keep it for
"someday."  It was useless, not even an antique, nor
did it qualify (yet) as a family keepsake.  Still . . .
turning it over in my hand I mused that it *was* kind of
pretty.  And, although currently my children wouldn't
willingly eat anything that contains even a drop of
vinegar, they might like to have it, someday.  Hard to
believe that I had wrapped it and packed it, then un-
wrapped it and put it away every time we had moved.
For twenty-one years.  I sighed and put the cruet back.

The coffee mug I pulled out next brought back
memories.  I had gotten it for Michael when we were
dating.  It's blue plaid pattern reminded me of his
favorite shirt.  The handle had been glued back on and
it had a small crack.  I doubted if it would hold water.
I also doubted if I'd ever get rid of it.  Back it went.

The next item qualified as "unidentifiable," made
of clay, painted brown with kind of greenish spots.
Before I could dispose of it, my older child swept it

away murmuring, "I wondered where that was!" I knew it would reappear one day — in the clutter on her dresser, or the clutter in the bathroom, or the jungle of clutter under her bed. And I knew I would probably then return it to the clutter in the kitchen cabinet. So be it.

It seems that simplifying is not so simple after all. Perhaps I need to redefine my terms. I think I was confusing "useful" with "value." I measured the items I came across against those practical, "useful" items in my vacation kitchen. But, now that I think about it, those things had no personality, no stories behind their purchase or use. They belonged to any and every family that stayed there. And they belonged to none. Our cabinet contains objects of use only to my family, whether we use them or not. Therefore, they have value.

My kitchen, despite my efforts, remains cluttered. A sure sign that my life is cluttered, I suppose. But it's the clutter of a busy family with a history. It's a collection of shared memories and stories, most of which are good (with the exception of that awful doctor in Florida). And I can live with that. Simple.

# Diet Books Don't Work

      I feel the need to alert the public to an alarming trend.  This is not a new trend, but it seems to have reached a fevered pitch.  I am referring to the "purchasing of diet books" trend.  There are now thousands of such publications available.  So many, in fact, that bookstores have actually made "Diet" a shelving category.  Titles such as *Diets Don't Work*, *Fit for Life*, and *The Last Diet You'll Ever Need* are selling like, well, like rice cakes.

      And everyone is jumping onto the chuck wagon — from doctors to singers to models to television talk-show hosts — they are all coming out of the woodwork attempting to feed the public's apparently insatiable desire to buy books about losing weight. Even Oprah Winfrey, who always seemed to me to be such a sensible person, has published a wildly popular tome called *Making the Connection: Ten Steps to a Better Body and a Better Life.* Now, while I certainly have no intention of divulging the secrets of this particular treatise, I will attempt to give you just a small preview of a few of the steps:

1. Make millions of dollars by having an immensely successful television talk show that allows you to —
2. go to a very expensive health spa where you can —
3. convince the chef to leave and become your own personal cook and help you write a best-selling cookbook so you can —
4. make millions of more dollars and then —
5. go to another exclusive spa where you get to —
6. convince the exercise guru to leave and become your own personal trainer and help you write a best-selling exercise book so you can —
7. make millions of more dollars.

For the rest of the steps to a better life, you will simply have to read the book in the bookstore coffee shop like I did.

I have also been intrigued with the highly marketed *Stop the Insanity* publication by Susan Powter. Frankly, I find this title curious because simply by looking at the book's cover it is obvious that this woman has not taken her own advice. How can I be expected to take seriously a woman who cuts her hair to within one-eighth of an inch of its life, dyes it white, and then exhorts me to, and this is a quote, "Eat, breath, and move"? During my extensive study of this book (which did not include actually reading it), I happened to catch the author on the Larry King Live Show wherein Mr. King, as always, asked the question that was on all of America's minds, to wit: "I beg your pardon? That's it? Eat, breath, move, that's all?" And Ms. Powter replied, with utmost sincerity, "Well, Larry, no one has ever told us to do those things before!" She has a point — and with that haircut, it shows.

Unfortunately, I was not able to stay with the show for the viewer call-in portion (well, it was time for *Quantum Leap)* but I am certain that the calls must have come from an appalled public, outraged, as am I, that this person, along with hundreds of others, is managing to take the simple, homespun advice our mothers gave us, to eat less and move more, turn it into 300 pages, and rake in billions of our dollars. I am confident that the Larry King Live telephone lines were jammed with calls from a public horrified, as am I, at the blatant manipulation of human suffering for profit, and a public dismayed, as am I, that they didn't think of it first.

But, after all, this is America, and you have to admit that these American authors have been able to achieve the most cherished dream of our founding fathers. Our ancestors embarked upon the perilous journey to the New World with one purpose, one goal, a single precious hope for their descendants. And I am certain that our forefathers and foremothers would be gratified to know that these authors have made that dream a reality. Because they are, in the most literal sense, living off the fat of the land.

# The Back Seat – Where It's At

$\mathscr{L}$ have been following with interest the discussions over the apparent dangers of the use of air bag restraints in automobiles. As a mother, I am in total agreement that people should be made aware of the risks of buckling small children into the front seat where an air bag could inflate with results too horrible to imagine. I don't know what the statistics are on this happening but certainly one instance is too many. So our government agencies, along with car manufacturers, are beginning to warn the public of the danger. In this effort, the National Safety Council (NSC), the National Highway Traffic Safety Administration (NHTSA), the National Transportation

Safety Board (NTSB), and local car dealers (LCD) have all joined together (which would make it the NSCNHTSANTSBLCD). They have begun an Air Bag Safety Campaign, featuring "**A B C** — **A**ir bag safety: **B**uckle everyone! **C**hildren in back!" We have recently received their package at our house. It includes a letter from our car dealer, a flyer containing the **A B C** information, a photograph of a happy child, safely buckled into the back seat of an automobile, and stickers to put in the window of the car to remind us to buckle our children in the back. Serious presentation, good, understandable information, simple plan. Kudos to the NSCNHTSANTSBLCD!

There are some car manufacturers, however, who have decided to do their own thing. One car company, for example, has just announced a program designed to encourage children to *want* to ride in the relatively safer back seat of the car. Unlike our government's more basic approach, this marketing plan is — how should I put this — totally inane.

This company (which shall remain nameless) has created a tag-line, guaranteed to appeal to America's youth — to their sense of hip, cool, not to mention way-out manner of speaking. They have created the following saying: "The back seat . . . that's where it's at!" This will probably be printed on posters, billboards, bumper stickers and splashed through Saturday morning television in an attempt to install a strong desire for the back seat into the psyches of our children.

I must say this slogan ranks right up there with some of the finer sayings ever composed, such as, "Drugs . . . they're what you just better not do!" and "Sex . . . that's what you really shouldn't think of until after you're married!"

One thing is clear to me. No one at this car company's marketing division has children. Because if they did, they would know that sitting in the front window seat is a privilege that has been coveted by squabbling siblings ever since the invention of the first four wheels. Why? *Because there is only one.* And any time you have only one of a thing — be it a front window seat, a lint-covered mint, or a dried-up magic marker — children will vie for it as if it were the only thing on earth that could possibly make them happy. It is the nature of the beast.

I would like to give this program benefit of the doubt, however. I am a mother, but it's possible I may not know everything. So I gave it a trial run with my own daughters. Following is the actual, unedited dialogue that transpired:

**First Child:**          "I call shotgun!"

**Second Child:**       "You can't! You had it last
                                 time!"

| | |
|---|---|
| **First Child:** | "Did not!" |
| **Second Child:** | "Did too!  Mom!" |
| **Mom, cheerfully:** | "The back seat . . . that's where it's at!" |
| **First Child:** | "Huh?  Where *what's* at?" |
| **Mom, patiently:** | "You know, *it*. Like the *cool it.* The place to be!" |
| **Second Child:** | "The place to be *what?*" |
| **Mom, desperately:** | "Gee, honey, don't you want to be where *it's at?*" |
| **Second Child:** | "*Whatever*!  Hey, move it!  I said it's my turn!  MOM!" |
| **First Child:** | "I called it first!  MOM!" |
| **Mom, grimly:** | "*Just get in the car!*" |

So the automobile companies are going to have to do better than:  "The back seat . . . that's where it's at!"  Today's younger generation just cannot be cajoled away from the front that easily.  If they really want to make the back seat "where it's at," they'd do well to answer my daughter's question:  "Where *what's* at?"  In other words, put something back there that will make it worth abandoning the age-old dispute for the front.  A few suggestions spring to this mother's mind:

- Install TVs and VCRs into the back of all vehicles, as standard equipment.  And no speakers, only earphones that don't reach the front.

- Build video games into the back of the front seats (like the ones on airplanes, except these should work).  Again, with earphones so parents don't go mad from the techno-noise (I'm sure more than one beeping computer game has caused more than one parent to drive into more than one tree!).
- Stop vehicles at random and give children "caught riding in the back" prizes.  Who would do the stopping?  How about automobile company marketing people?  They seem to have a lot of time on their hands.

Or they could make the front seats safer. Now there's a thought.  I know they are working on this,but a few more ideas certainly couldn't hurt:

- Put swivel seats on the front passenger side. Seats that can be turned and locked to face the back.  That way, when the child is buckled in, he/she is safe from the sudden inflation of an air bag, mom can reach the child if necessary, and the child can then more effectively torment his/her siblings.
- Install a computer chip that automatically disen-gages the air bag system if the person in the passenger seat is under a certain weight.  If they can make a chip that monitors the level of wind-shield washing fluid, they can make a chip to do this.

In the end, of course, it's the parents who determine where their children are going to ride in the car. More than once I have heard someone say that she doesn't always belt her child in because "He just doesn't like being strapped down and I get tired of fighting. Besides, I'm a good driver." Of course, good drivers have accidents all the time.

I do empathize with the frustration, however. When my children were little and fought being put into their carseats (as many do), I saw a photograph in *Parent* magazine — a mother buckling in a highly uncooperative baby — with a caption that read, "Even if she protests, be firm. Remember, *you* are the mom." For some reason, that small item gave me the confidence to insist that my children be as safe as possible in our car. Somehow, we need to make parents realize that they are, after all, in charge. And all the marketing in the world can't take the place of that.

# Y2K or YNOT2K, That Is The Problem

$\mathscr{L}$ must admit I am concerned about the "Y2K problem." Every day there is another article or radio program featuring experts making dire predictions and giving advice for dealing with Y2K. For those of you who immediately turn to the entertainment section or the oldies station, I will explain Y2K to you in easy, unambiguous terms. Basically "Y2K" is a cute acronym for "The End Of the World." At midnight on December 31, 1999, all of the computers on earth will stop working. Businesses will shut down, airplanes will fall from the sky, banks will have no records of your money, and, worst of all, internet chat rooms will disappear. Why? Because our technology forefathers designed computers so that they could only count *up.* From the 1950s to the '60s, to the '70s and so forth up to '99. Then, because they were programed to read just the last two digits, when the year 2000 (Y2K, get it?) rolls around, the poor things will not recognize the '00 as a positive number and will calculate everything as a negative, which will confuse programs. Confused computer programs behave much like confused people. They do nothing. Thus the catastrophic consequences above. Why, you may ask, were computer designers so short-sighted? As one computer pioneer remarked, "Who knew the world would last so long?"

So what can be done? Well, we could take the advice of the above high-tech experts. Unfortunately, because they are high-tech experts and we are not high-tech listeners, the issue is further confused. A typical expert's suggestion: "Consumers should check with their financial institutions to determine what strategies are in place for the upcoming potential Y2K problems."

Now, there are at least two things wrong with this advice. First, it assumes that consumers have *any clue* what a Y2K strategy for financial institutions should be. As far as I can tell, my own financial institution doesn't even have a strategy for finding a check I wrote months ago, which was cashed, but hasn't shown up on my statement. Forget "upcoming potential problems." Most consumers are pretty busy with current real problems.

Secondly, how would that conversation go?

"Good morning, First State Second National Federal Peoples Citizens City Bank, your place for loans, mortgages, nearly free checking and cool safety deposit boxes. How may I assist you?"

"Yes, I would like to inquire about the bank's strategy for Y2K, please."

"I beg your pardon?"

"The Y2K problem. I'd like to know what your institution is planning to do about it."

"Y2K? Um . . . one moment please."

(Ten minutes of muzak version of "Don't Worry, Be Happy")

"Ma'am, is that anything like a 401(K)?"

So I honestly don't believe that this is particularly useful advice from our high-tech expert. I fear that we're pretty much on our own here. Therefore, I have set up my own strategy for Y2K. I plan to:

1. Take all of my money out of the bank and stuff it under my bed;

2. Run hard copies of all information on my computer. Then, back up all of my computer records on disks. Stuff copies and disks under my bed;

3. Spend New Year's Eve, 1999, under my bed.

You may, of course, follow my example. It might be best, however, if you use your own bed. Good luck in the new millennium.

# How to Sell Your House

$\mathcal{L}$et's face it, the selling of your home is one of the most stressful events that you can voluntarily bring upon yourself.  In fact, as stress indicators are measured, "change in residence" is right up there with "loss of a loved one" and "loss of employment" (which are not normally considered voluntary events). I have taken it upon myself, strictly as a public service, to do a little research on the subject. Between thinking a lot about it and talking to people in line at the grocery store, I have come to the following conclusions:  1.  No one should ever move; and, 2.  People in grocery store lines have very little patience and practically no sense of humor.  However, if you feel you must make a residential adjustment in your life, I strongly suggest you consider the following:

**Is this move really necessary?** Too many people make the unfortunate decision to move when staying put is the obvious better choice. Before becoming another sad statistic, review the problems you have with your current residence and try to find creative alternative solutions. Following are some suggestions to tackle common problems:

**Problem:** Current house is too small for a growing family.

**Solution:** Have fewer children.

**Problem:** The roof/basement/entire house leaks/leans/is completely falling apart.

**Solution:** Not to worry! All homes have small problems such as these. It's part of their charm! Why go through all of the hassle of selling your home when all it needs is a little TLC? If you feel something *must* be done, then you can send away for a set of those "Handyman's Do-It-Yourself" videos (set of 25 at $99.95 each), purchase the required tools (set of 347 at $79.95 each), and those pesky repair problems will be a thing of the past! Of course, you will also need to get a "yard barn" for your workshop (set of one at $4,000 each — $7,000 if assembled) and will probably

need to quit your job in order to have time to do
the work.

**Problem:**  Neighborhood is being overrun by
criminals, drug dealers, and/or religious fanatics.

**Solution:**  Basically, these situations should be
looked upon as opportunities for creativity!  Set up
your own neighborhood "protection agency."  Have
bake sales and car washes to raise money.  Then
use the money to dispatch the religious fanatics to
the homes of the criminals and drug dealers.  This
will move them out *much* faster than any violent
approach ever could!  You might want to look
around for some insurance salespeople as well.

**Problem**:  Local school system is worse than local
prison system.

**Solution**:  Don't be too concerned.  No doubt your
children will very likely benefit from both.

**Problem**:  Getting divorced.

**Solution**:  Simply because your marriage has expired,
there is no reason to sell the house!  All you need is
some good strong electrician's tape.  Split the
house down the center and you can each live on
your own side (in the case of a less-than-amicable
divorce, you might consider an "invisible fence;"
shock collars could well become the newest fashion
accessories).  You can have the bathroom on
Mondays, Wednesdays, and Fridays and your

ex-spouse gets to use it on Tuesdays, Thursdays, and Saturdays. The kids can have Sundays (they never wash, brush, or flush anyway). Small compromises such as these can save you an enormous amount of time, trouble, and money.

**Problem**: We just really, really, really want to move.

**Solution**: No, you really, really, really don't.

After all of the above considerations are weighed, I'm sure you have a bundle of reasons to stay right where you are. No? You've decided to sell your home anyway? No doubt a huge mistake, but who am I to judge? I continue my investigation of the best ways for you to go about this enormous task. I will, however, need to find new subjects to interview because my local grocery store has strongly suggested I take my business elsewhere.

After having weighed all of the pros and cons of moving and after inexplicably having decided to sell anyway, the next step is:

***Determine whether to sell "by owner" or hire a real estate agent.*** Before you decide to attempt to sell your house "by owner" — note the word "attempt" — ask yourself these three important questions:

1. Am I willing to give up all evenings and weekends for the next two or three years in this attempt?
2. Do I have any knowledge/expertise/credentials in

the real estate business (having been on the buying or selling end of a residential real estate transaction does *not* qualify here)?

AND/OR

3.  Do I have any close family or friends with the above knowledge/expertise/credentials (who would not also expect to be paid)?

If you answered "No" to these key questions, you should call a professional realtor immediately — do not pass "Go," do not pay $200 application fee. This advice comes from vast negative experience. When we, a family of four highly intelligent individuals (six, if you count the dogs), decided to sell our own home, we naturally thought it was so unique, charming, and marketable that people would be lining up to throw money at us for it. So confident were we that we simply went to the hardware store and bought a "For Sale by Owner" sign and stuck it in the front yard. It didn't take long for us to realize that there is a bit more to it than that. People began to ask how much we wanted for the house. This, we felt, was a real good question. And this leads us to our next invaluable hint:

**Decide how much you want for your house.** Despite what real estate professionals would have you believe, determining a price for your home is not difficult. Simply estimate the amount you would hope to get for your house, then subtract $50,000.  At least that's how we did it — although it took us *much* longer.

After you have settled on the "asking price" (this is just one of the many technical real estate terms with which you will become nauseatingly familiar during the next few weeks, months, or possibly years), notify your agent and when he/she stops laughing, you will be ready for the next phase:

***Prepare your home for the market.*** This is a necessary and extremely humbling aspect of the process.  Your real estate agent will let you know what you need to do to make your home more market-able.  Try to hold your tongue when your agent suggests that you deep-six the huge oil painting of Grandpa Harry in his Model T that has been over the couch since you were married.  They may not be interior decorators, but they know ugly.

Along these same lines, we offer the following advice to assist you in putting your home in prime condition, ready to be seen by prospective buyers.

The first step in preparation for "showings" — another technical term — is to seriously *clean up your house!* You would be amazed at how many people neglect this important step.  When we were looking at homes, we were astonished at the wretched condition of many of the homes we visited.  Based on our extensive research we have determined that many people are not as, shall we say, fastidious as we would hope. It is not that difficult to prepare your home for potential buyers. A few simple pointers:

1. Remove the Christmas decorations (unless it is within one week either side of the actual holiday). Please, there is nothing more depressing than a tree with no needles left and dried up mistletoe in June! And turn off the piped-in carols even if it *is* Christmas!

2. Get rid of your dirty laundry. Failure to do this will make a highly negative impression. Stepping over piles of smelly socks and underwear — especially in the living room — tends to make one wonder if the plumbing and electrical systems have been properly maintained. Have some pride! Make sure your dirty laundry is not lying about! As we mentioned previously, we put ours in the trunk of our car. Alternatively, you might take it all to a relative's for the duration. Or, you might consider actually putting it into the washer and/or dryer, if there's room.

3. Try to avoid making sauerkraut on the day of a showing. Do not cook fish again until after the closing.

4. Get rid of any animals. Sure your kids love them, but where are your priorities? I'm not suggesting you kill them or anything, just find a temporary

loving home that's not for sale.  If any of your
relatives are still speaking to you after the laundry
thing, try them.

5. Don't leave bananas out on the counter.  We don't
   know why, but that's what our agent told us.
   Perhaps a lot of prospective buyers steal bananas.

6. Clear out storage spaces.  Go through all of your
   closets, pantries, attics, etc., and clear out *everything* — all leftover college/new marriage furniture,
   all unused wedding presents, all clothing you think
   will come back in style, all heirlooms from relatives
   with bad taste, and, yes, the record albums —
   everything.  You want to give the impression that
   there is so much storage room in this house, that
   you can't *possibly* begin to fill it.

7. Do not have a garage sale!  After you have
   completed the previous step, you are probably
   thinking, "Look at all of this stuff!  What a good
   time to have a garage sale!"  Right?  *Wrong!*  This is
   an enormous mistake commonly made by the
   novice homeseller.  Do not allow yourself to fall into
   this trap!  Under no circumstances do you want a
   newspaper ad inviting just anyone to your home!
   Remember this time-honored business rule:  *When
   you invite the public, the public tends to show up.*
   Trust me, this is rarely a good thing.  Invest in a
   month-by-month storage unit and put all of the

above mentioned junk in it. If you're lucky you will forget it's there.

8. Take a close look at the outside of your house. Real estate professionals refer to this as "curb appeal," but they're not really talking about the curb. Believe it or not, prospective buyers often get their first impression of your house by pulling up in front and looking at it. Your job is to see to it that they don't immediately pull away, leaving unsightly skid marks on the street. Think about the front of your house. Is it appealing? Grass and flowers are a good idea. If you discover that your home is not in a very attractive spot/ neighborhood/city, you might consider having the house moved to a more desirable location.

Now your house is ready! It looks better now than it did when you bought it! Are you crazy? Why would anyone sell such a beautiful place? Okay, okay, just trying to help. The next step is to get through the showings themselves, preferably without pharmaceutical help. Now it's time to:

**Bring on the prospective buyers!** Yes, folks, the time has now come to allow — even *encourage* — total strangers to wander through your most private spaces, making judgments about your taste in furniture, decorating, stereo equipment, peeking into drawers and closets, and discussing your lifestyle

with other total strangers.  But don't worry, you won't
be there to hear their snide remarks and smug
comments.  And you're far too classy a person to
place a small tape recorder under a bed (on top of the
refrigerator is a good spot, also)!  Unfortunately, you
also won't be there to defend yourself ("Heh, heh, it's
a funny story how that hole got in the wall there . . .").
But don't worry, your realtor will make a full report to
you after each showing.  One small warning, though:
Do not take anything anyone may say about your
house personally.  For instance, we had a family who
didn't like our house because it was too clean!  One
woman wasn't interested because she didn't like our
dog (actual quote:  "Why don't they have something
small — like a poodle?").  Another person even
complained about the number of rooms — she said
she got lost during the showing.

Either your house will say "home" to someone,
or it won't.  And if it doesn't, folks have to find a
reason why it doesn't.  If they can't think of something logical (and most can't), they will come up with
something ludicrous (another actual quote:  "This
house smells funny.  Don't it smell funny, Doris?").
People are not rational beings.  Always keep that in
mind.

In the end, you will very likely find someone
who will give you an offer on your home.  At that time,

you have to be willing to commit to move out. They
tend to insist. And the process of looking for, finding,
and purchasing a new home is another subject
altogether. And thinking about it just makes me want
to lie down.

One last thought: Although following the above
advice will help prepare you and your house for
prospective buyers, it will not guarantee that the sale
of your home will be problem-free. In fact, the *only*
guarantee in this whole process is that you *will have*
enormous, frustrating, ulcer-producing, mind-numb-
ing problems! But that doesn't mean it can't be fun!
Remember — attitude is *everything*. When you find
yourself saying, "Someday we're going to laugh about
this," why wait? After all, this is serious business,
but it need not be dismal. This is not a job — it's an
adventure! Happy house hunting!

# Rejection

No one likes to be rejected. Rejection is especially painful for those of us who are offering our creative efforts, much like beloved children, for scrutiny. For fledgling writers, such as myself, it is at first thrilling to receive rejections — however imper-sonal — from newspapers, magazines, book publish-ers, etc. Receiving a rejection notice means that someone actually received, handled, perhaps even read my work! I have collected all of the rejections I have received. I consider them to be symbols of my status as a "real" writer. As the impersonal, unsigned form letters began to pile up, however, the novelty began to wear a little thin and disappointment and frustration set in.

I realize, of course, that publishers are constantly inundated with tons of material, and I understand that form letters are necessary in order to deal with the deluge (truly I do). Still, after a while, it began to hurt. And before too long, I started to doubt my choice of a writing career and to question my talent. My resolve began to erode, and a good, solid depression snuck up on me with an accompanying writer's block.

Rather than sit back and take it, allowing self-pity to set in (the eighth deadly sin, as you know), I decided, for my own sanity, I must have a modest amount of revenge. Not really revenge, so much as the last word. So I created the following letter and sent it to each company that rejected my material.

I would like to be able to tell you that one of the offending organizations called me, apologized, and immediately offered me a contract. But that didn't happen. So I have to comfort myself that, perhaps, someone read the letter, got the joke and smiled while throwing it away. Small comfort, but comfort nevertheless.

Dear Editorial Department:

I have received your rejection of my submission to your organization. Please excuse this form letter, but the quantity of rejections that I receive does not permit me to reply individually. I read your rejection with interest and feel it has some merit. Each rejection is carefully considered and I certainly appreciate the effort that goes into every rejection sent. Due to the vigorous competition for a chance to reject my material, it is necessary to carefully select those I can accept. Unfortunately, your rejection just does not meet my current needs. Therefore, I'm afraid I cannot accept your rejection at this time.

Thank you so much for your rejection. It may be just right for another author at another time. I hope you will not become discouraged. You may well have the opportunity to reject future material I may send you.

Most Sincerely,

Kathleen F. Rhodes